Why Are They Like That? Hispanics

Questions you've dared to ask, answered by real people, celebrities and experts

A book series based on the award-winning sharing project that's captured worldwide attention helping people in their personal, social and business relationships

Phillip J. Milano

For Robin, Jacob, Lucas and Ben

Publisher:
Y Forum
yforum@yforum.com

ISBN: 978-1-07-933346-6

Cover and interior layout by Sandy Weber,
Key 3 Creative, Jacksonville, Florida
Cover photo credit: Rawpixel. Stock photo for illustrative purposes
only; any person depicted is a posed model.

Content based in part on the popular Y? sharing project and Dare
to Ask column

Find out more about the author, upcoming books and speeches at
www.phillipmilano.com, www.facebook.com/PhillipJMilano or
@PhillipMilano.

Books In This Series

Why Are They Like That? Blacks

Why Are They Like That? Whites

Why Are They Like That? Hispanics

Why Are They Like That? Asians

Why Are They Like That? Gay Men

Why Are They Like That? Lesbians

Why Are They Like That? Women

Why Are They Like That? Men

Why Are They Like That? Rich and Poor

Why Are They Like That? Religious (or not)

Why Are They Like That? Disabled People

Why Are They Like That? Young and Old

Praise for the Y? sharing project and the book "I Can't Believe You Asked That!" (Perigee)

"Milano is quietly revolutionizing cross-cultural communication..."
- Pulitzer Prize-winning columnist Leonard Pitts

"If you've ever hesitated to ask a question because you think it might be considered insensitive or impolitic, now is your chance ... Nothing is considered out of bounds..."
- CNN Headline News

"(It) tells more about who we are and how we feel about each other than you're likely to learn from a dozen sociology texts…"
- Washington Post News Service

"Mr. Milano has dared to open the field of debate to the maximum…"
- Le Monde, Paris

"(A) remarkable contribution to cross-cultural understanding…"
- The (London) Guardian

"A truly rare achievement … has the potential to have a profound impact on the way we all see and understand each other..."
- Playboy magazine

"It's an incredible book. It diffuses everything ... Nothing is off limits, and the questions have that childlike honesty to them..."
- Dee Snider, Twisted Sister; host, "Dee Snider Radio"

"A take-no-prisoners attitude prevails between the volume's covers . . . This book is hard to put down..."
- Midwest Book Review

"A+ (highest rating) … Everything you wanted to know but were afraid to ask gets tackled here ..."
- Entertainment Weekly

4

CONTENTS

Introduction

Why Are They Like That? is a series of books based on an award-winning worldwide sharing project in which real people, experts and celebrities talk about things that make us different from each other. Silly things. Sad things. Funny things. Profound things.

Read with an open mind and we believe that by the time you're finished you'll have a much better understanding of how to make more and real friends, money and love. It's that simple.

Why? Because this isn't about trying to get ahead with diversity training. We are well beyond that. According to the Census Bureau, by 2050 the United States will have no racial or ethnic minority.

No, this is about moving past talking about how to understand each other to talking to each other. Right now.

That's why there's no agenda to these books other than getting the conversation going. We can discuss studies and methods for elevating social consciousness all we want, but there is no substitute for real dialogue.

That's where Why Are They Like That? stands apart from other books on the topic. You will see how people talk about their real differences of race, religion, sex, disability and more.

The success of the approach is proven: It's based on the ground-breaking Y? website project, blog and column that have attracted millions of visitors and worldwide media attention.

Our hope is that by reading, you will become more comfortable asking and answering the questions yourself, expecting the unexpected in return and helping change the ground rules for how we learn from and about each other. To that end, we wrap up each book in the series with our O.U.T.L.O.U.D. Method for Dialogue, with tips to help you get your own conversations started. Ultimately, that is what this effort is all about.

After all, if you want to make more friends, money and love, you better know the people you're talking to, selling to or opening to. Knowledge isn't just power. It's all power.

Enjoy.

Phillip J. Milano
Founder, Y?

Do stuffed animals decorate the hearts of Latinos?

They asked:

There are more Latinos moving into our community. ... In several homes I have visited there have been several large stuffed animals on display. Why are these used as prominent decorative pieces?

— *Candice, 25, white, Fremont, Neb.*

You said:

I've always associated adults with stuffed toys as something young white women sometimes have a thing for, as a way of playfully showing they haven't yet needed to grow up because their families are so well-off. Sounds to me like what you're assuming is something a few Latinos do is actually more a sign of upper middle-class assimilation or imitating well-off white women.

— *A.C.C., 34, Mexican and American Indian male, Indiana*

This generally lower-middle-class white lesbian has about 30 stuffed animals in her living room.

— *Alma, 46, white, Texas*

I guess we just like to decorate our houses with inexpensive items. Sometimes you'll see clown and circus animal statuettes; sometimes you'll see little plastic dolls from 25-cent vending machines; sometimes you'll see empty tequila bottles lined up on the mantle, etc. It has a folksy, kitschy charm.

— *Dan, 21, Latino, Los Angeles*

We found:

Just so no says we stuffed the ballot box, we're having a good ol' Caucasian designer weigh in on this one, as well as a Latina. Two folks with more taste than most of us, for the price of one.

Emmy-winning interior decorator Christopher Lowell, who's hosted Discovery Channel's "It's Christopher Lowell," is one of the originators of the "turnaround" -- he goes into homes of folks of modest means and offers to spruce up their decor on a budget.

When low-income Hispanics decorate with stuffed animals, it's often about trying to "hang on" to something, he said.

"When I ask them about it, it's about displacement. Because of vacillating immigration laws, and with some being illegal, especially among females, these little characters are the equivalent of imaginary friends," he said. Many outgrow the stuffed characters, or they may save a few in a curio cabinet.

"They become like diary benchmarks — these stuffed toys may have been taken with them at one time, maybe even on the run," said Lowell, who hosts "Ask Christopher" at christopherlowell.com.

All in all, he said, much of it has to do with cultural inheritance — in the same way some Hispanics use bright colors to celebrate their homelands, or some Italian-Americans put slip-covers on their furniture out of a poverty-consciousness.

Marlene Pratt, a second-generation Cuban-Dominican interior designer who's co-hosted Univision's "Mi Casa es Su Casa" and co-founded casalatina.com, said she's seen the stuffed animals among Hispanics and other cultures.

"If you walk into a first-generation Italian home and they are attached to something like that, they aren't going to let go of it. If you walk into an Irish home and see it, they won't want to let go."

She helps people see things in a different way from the past.

She said some stereotypes — such as slip-covers on Italian-American sofas — are just that.

"Ha, my mother had plastic on her furniture, too. I pushed her to take it off. I had to sign a paper that stated that if the sofa got stained or fell apart, I would have to buy a new sofa."

Who's speaking the 'right' Spanish: Spaniards or Latinos?

They asked:

Do Spaniards view Latinos as butchering the Spanish language?
— *Ridley, 22, white male, Chambersburg, Penn.*

You said:

I don't think South Americans are butchering Spanish, but I find it irritating when South Americans refer to themselves as "Spanish."
— *Jade, 16, Spanish, Australia*

I'm from Venezuela, and when we talk to North Americans or Europeans, we never refer to ourselves as Spanish; actually, we hate when somebody says we are "Spanish" — we say Venezuelan or Colombianos, etc.
— *Monica, 15, Caracas, Venezuela*

There is a big difference in Castilian Spanish and the dialects in Latin America, and even within Spain. Just like in the United States with a person from New York trying to talk to a person from New Orleans.
— *Frank, 34, Hispanic, Denver*

Unfortunately, some folks from Spain do think that Latin Americans don't speak properly. But the same thing happens within Spain.
— *Angela, Georgia*

Spaniards, especially ones using the Castilian dialect, sound like Elmer Fudd [Editor's note: make that Daffy Duck] to me. They use a "th" sound in place of all the "s" sounds: Buenath diath thenor. Sometimes it's hard for me to keep a straight face.
— *A.C.C., Mexican and American Indian male, Phoenix*

You're wrong. In the "Castilian" dialect as you call it, no one says Buenath diath — not only because dia is masculine and so would take buenos — but also because the "th" sound is only used for "z" and "c" when followed by "e" or "i."

— *Maria, Hispanic, United Kingdom*

We found:

Some Spaniards do tend to look down on Latin Americans — even using the nasty racial slur *sudaca* to refer to South American immigrants, said Professor Dan Greenberg, director of Latin American Studies at Pace University in New York. Some of the mistreatment comes from being confronted with people perceived as "different," and often "what marks you is the way you talk."

"There is a lot of mean harassment," he said. "Spaniards in general have always taken a superior attitude toward Latins. ... Spain has moved forward culturally, but old attitudes die hard."

Some of the language differences are because Spanish evolved as its use grew in Latin America. For example, Mexicans use a more syncopated rhythm when they talk, Greenberg said. And *Lunfardo*, a street slang that started with the poor, underworld and prostitutes, is spoken in places like Buenos Aires and can be hard to grasp for an average Spanish speaker.

As far as jabs about Spaniards talking "funny": In Castilian Spanish, spoken in central and northern Spain, they do pronounce "c" and "z" as "th."

"Some think they have a lisp problem, but they are just correctly pronouncing those letters that way, in that language," Greenberg said.

Are black people *personas non grata* with Latinos?

They asked:

I am Latina and have dated outside my race, particularly black males. ... I've never been mistreated by blacks; I received only positive vibes. From my own community, I was criticized and harassed and called names. What have been other Latinos' experiences?

— Raquel, 31, Gary, Ind.

You said:

Hispanics and blacks have animosity toward each other, and the males of any race feel degraded and rejected when the females of their race are dating the supposed "enemy."

— Eric, 22, Hispanic, Riverside, Calif.

Don't give me that shit, that only the Hispanic culture does not accept interracial dating, dude. You are full of yourself, clean it up. America is not color blind yet.

— Latino, 30, male, Virginia

I'm dating a Hispanic. As soon as we're around Hispanics, they stare and make comments, quite often in Spanish. My girlfriend won't translate for me because she knows it'll probably lead to a fight.

— Dirk, 23, white, Houston

It appears there's a little uneasiness in the homefront. ... There seems to be resistance to change in everyone. We can hold on until we choke the life out of something. It is sad.

— Virlyn, 42, black female, Flint, Mich.

Mira muchacha -- have more consideration when talking about your race. "Positive vibes" don't come from one race.

— Amanda, 18, Hispanic, Bristol, Penn.

We found:

Antes de que pienses mal — and don't go loco on us, either — it's this guy below saying this stuff, not us. He's smart and Latino.

Right or wrong, it's like this:

Latinos who are prejudiced tend to be less so against blacks than against Anglos, said psychologist Samuel Roll, co-author of "The Invisible Border: Latinos in America." But it's not always a lovefest with blacks.

"Colonialism and slavery leave a residue, and part of it is disdain for people who've been abused," said Roll, professor emeritus at the University of New Mexico.

Black people remain at the bottom of the social ladder in America, despite their achievements and despite President Obama, he said.

"We try to pretty that over, but it's hard to be black. Immigrants struggling to make it might feel their kids are associating with a lower caste, and the family doesn't want that."

Also, the extended family is huge in Latino culture.

"If someone is threatening family unity, it's like, 'How far away from us is he going to take you?' " Roll said.

But mostly it's fear, real or not, of being held back.

"It's 'You're going to hurt our grandchildren by making them the kind of people treated like shit in this country," he said. "It's painful to be black. One patient told me, 'I'm over hating being black, but sometimes I wish I could just pull off my black skin, so when I go up to a counter and am not treated first, I don't have to think it's because I'm black.' "

She's ready to say 'Adios' to this language trend

They asked:

Is anyone else offended by the United States being taken over by the Spanish language? Customer service lines ask you to "Press 1 for English" — why?

— Glenda, 26, black, Cincinnati

You said:

I agree. The same government that overlooks illegal Spanish immigrants is the same one giving them rights. It's all politics.

— Peter, 21, black, Jacksonville

Really refreshing to know you speak Native American fluently since you live here.

— Daryl, 30, Asian, Texas

I completely agree. Now they want to make it a requirement in our schools that the children need to take up the language. What is wrong with making them who come into our country learn our language, English?

— Rhea, 22, white, Albany, N.Y.

"Taken over"? Giving people an option on a phone line means being taken over?

— Amy, 42, white, Philadelphia

We found:

Welcome to the "Why Are They Like That?" Debate. Our official rules: The "Spanish is OK" guy and the "but English is more OK" lady below each have 14 seconds to make a point.

Mr. Juan Tornoe, owner of market research firm Hispanic Trending and an international consultant, your opening statement, please:

"It's only a very small minority that are not ever learning English. They want to learn. But there's a period of time when you come here and just don't know English ... so it makes business sense to offer services in English and Spanish."

Ms. Raegan Baker of the non-profit ProEnglish, which works to make English the official language of the United States, your response?

"We need to be able to communicate with each other. Most countries have an official language. Countries with two or more languages are falling apart. In Belgium, they have French and Dutch. They are breaking apart."

Mr. Tornoe?

"Knowing more languages is better; it helps the brain develop more. You have more access to science, to literature, etc. ... If you go to Switzerland, they have three languages and aren't bickering about it. In Central and South America, people are speaking in English and Spanish. ... Here, it's a system that is not stimulating people to learn things outside of their own ZIP code. We get immersed in micro-communities and don't see what's going on outside."

Ms. Baker?

"At the government level, we want English as the official language ... Obviously if we have to do things like print ballots in more than one language, that costs taxpayers ... but the main thing is, it's hard to succeed if you don't learn English. We try to stress that we want immigrants, but they can't succeed if they can't communicate. And we want them to succeed."

We'll be back after these words from our sponsor, the entire financial system of China.

Crack one open and learn about Mexicans, beer and Sunday

They asked:

Why do Mexicans at grocery stores or mini-marts seem to always be buying huge packs of beer on Sunday afternoons?

— C., California

You said:

It's a long tradition related to soccer. On Sundays there's soccer games . . . and men get together to watch the game and have beer and food.

— J., Boston

Many Mexicans work on Saturdays, and Sunday is a family day. Many go to parks, BBQs and the beach.

— Michael, 23, Hispanic, Los Angeles

We are near a small village that is the nursery capital of the South. Many migrant workers live somewhere between here and there. Sundays are usually their only day off, and they come to town to eat at a restaurant, buy groceries and beer and pay their cell phone bills.

— Erica, white, Louisiana

If you think it's only a Mexican thing, you should see the Brits, Aussies and Kiwis I associate with on Sundays.

— Adrian, 36, white male, Hong Kong

Mexicans . . . have no one to go home to except for the other people that live in their trailer/apartment building and they want to get their fiesta on.

— Kyle, 15, white, Texas

Mexicans are some of the hardest workers I've ever known. ... I have always preferred to get drunk on Saturday. That way I could rest on Sunday and be ready to work on Monday. I have worked with a ton of Mexican guys, and it has always amazed me how they can get so drunk on Sunday night and then get up Monday morning and still pick twice as many peaches as I did.

— Ron S., 60, Stockton, Calif.

We found:

Alma R. Martinez is a Broadway and film actor whose film credits include "Born in East L.A." with Cheech and Chong and "Under Fire" with Nick Nolte, Gene Hackman and Ed Harris. The former theater professor at Pomona College in California also lectures about Latino stereotypes. She addressed some of the stuff tossed out by readers above.

Mexicans work on Saturdays: True for many in lower-income brackets, and not only that, many work two jobs. "My dad had three jobs at one point: in a garage in the day, at night grinding liver for [Eli] Lilly, and another job at a body shop."

Mexicans buy big packs of beer on Sundays: Well, Sundays are viewed as a day of rest, which goes back to Catholic traditions in Mexico. "You go to church, you do what you do, there are gatherings, weddings, and as far as beer, because Mexico in the north is very hot, you drink beer and Coca-Cola."

Mexicans work hard: "It's ridiculous to say we are lazy. Mexicans work hard at everything and are trying to send some of that money back home . . . they are working hard to support families."

Ron S. above gets drunk on Saturdays: We said she addressed some of the stuff.

Mexicans have no one (extended family-wise) to go home to: And that's why many hold gatherings on Sundays — often at free or inexpensive places like the beach or park. "We often don't have support from extended family in the U.S. . . . so what family and friends are here is important."

This look has pluck and says 'proud to be Latina'

They asked:

Why do a lot of Hispanic women pluck their eyebrows and then draw them on with an eyebrow pencil? And why do they draw a hard lip outline and paste their hair flat with gel? These appear harsh to me, but they must appear sexy to you and Hispanic men?

— Ellen, 48, white, Broomfield, Colo.

You said:

You answered your own question. Because that is what they think looks good. Beauty is in the eye of the beholder.

— Shelly, 49, white, New Alexandria, Pa.

I am a Hispanic female; however I do not pluck all my eyebrows and then draw them in with a pencil. That is a choice that different females make, Hispanic or not. I do on occasion draw a hard lip outline simply because I like how I look. I always "paste" my hair flat with gel, though, whenever I wear it up in a ponytail because I like to look neat and presentable and not like I just woke up . . . and didn't want to brush my hair. Believe it or not, it is hard work, especially since I have a lot of hair and it is way past my waist.

— Sandy, 20, Santa Cruz, Calif.

We found:

Say hola to the chola.

Chola girls, that is. They are primarily Latina teens (not all of them now, folks, just a small portion) in larger urban areas who have adopted a certain style, said Lorena Chinchilla, editor of Lindisima.com, the largest beauty Web site for Latinas in the U.S.

And what is that style?

18

Hmmm. To quote lyrics from "Lean like a Chola," West Coast radio personality Carmen's parody of the Chicano rap single "Lean Like a Cholo":

never mess with a chick, with lip liner no lipstick

wanna look good I'll tell you how

first gotta paint on your eyebrows

spray your hair with Aqua Net

get a tattoo to rep your set

What we have here is a look that came of age with "chola" girls who hung out with "cholos" (not always gang-bangers, but working-class, tough Latinos nonetheless), according to Chinchilla. It's a way they distinguish themselves, she said.

"It started out being associated with street gangs, but now it's more acceptable. You don't have to belong to a gang. It's just a way to stand out, to say 'I'm proud of being Latina.' "

Many cholas, or "cholitas," have adopted a more classic style now, but the harsher look is still around, more acceptable and mainstream. It was a look favored by pop singer Gwen Stefani (of Italian, Irish and Scottish descent, no less), complete with distinguishing high ponytail, hair gel, dark eyebrows, heavy lip-liner, etc.

While the makeup and clothing style — sometimes a tight top and bare midriff, with low-rise jeans, big earrings, Catholic-saint necklaces, expensive sneakers — can be off-putting to some, it's not about how others feel about it, Chinchilla said.

"Part of it is that cholas are just trying to belong to a group, so they are not necessarily saying [with their look] 'Don't mess with me' — although some of them do mean it."

In Mexico they can get pretty physical over nicknames

They asked:

Hispanics refer to me as "wedda." What does it mean?

— N.F., 44, white female, Denver

You said:

The word is huera and it's pronounced more like "where-a" or "where-o" (huero, to refer to a guy). It basically means "white girl" or "white guy" in a positive kind of way.

— FreedaBee, 42, white female, California

Actually, no. It's about as positive as if you had a Latino "friend" who you addressed as "spic" — but in a "playful" manner.

— Jill, Chicago

In Spain I learned huero means "empty" or "hollow" and is commonly used to refer to an unfertilized egg. Somehow huero came to describe a person who is "white with nothing inside."

— Teresa, white, Gurnee, Ill.

Don't take offense. Mexicans often refer to individuals by their characteristics. For example, blacks = "Negros," Asians = "Chinos," thin = "Flaco" and in my case, fat = "Gordo."

— Oscar, Mexican, Hawaii

Would this extend to physical abnormalities? For example, would someone in a wheelchair be called the Mexican equivalent of "cripple"?

— Marcia, 43, white, Venice

We found:

Wedda you (or your mudda or fadda) like it or not, if you're in rural Mexico or around lower-income or urban Mexican youths in the United States, you may get a nickname based on your physical features.

"There are communities in Mexico where no one knows the real name of the person," said Alexandro Jose Gradilla, chair of Chicano and Chicana studies at Cal State Fullerton. "For example, this one is 'the doll,' who is the brother of 'the skinny one,' who is getting married to 'the angry one.' Then you get a wedding invitation, and you're like 'Who is Jose Garcia and Susanna Gonzalez?' "

To refer to a fair-skinned person, it's guero or guera, or huero or huera. And yes, it would be deemed a term of endearment, Gradilla said.

"It's a way of being familiar. It sounds weird to American sensibilities, like why are you referring to my whiteness?"

Guera goes back to Mexico's colonial period, when Spaniards had a caste system in place that hinged on who was more "European" and who wasn't, which often meant who had lighter skin, he said.

"It's strange, in the United States we know about race, but we don't like talking about it . . . but in other countries you acknowledge the difference in the open."

Not all nicknames are "fun" — on some Latin-American Jerry Springer-type shows, the terms can seem pretty cold, Gradilla said.

"They'll be like, there's 'flat nose' — chato. But, it's like a bonding thing. If you don't have a nickname, you're kind of an outsider, so they are trying to make you feel part of the group when they do this. They are accepting something that we are supposed to ignore. It's calling out the elephant in the room."

No spin here about Hispanic spinsters

They asked:

Why do Hispanic women have to be married before they are in their 30s?

— K.C., Indianola, Miss.

You said:

In the eyes of many in the Hispanic culture, a woman without a man has less value.

— Monica, 27, Hispanic, San Antonio

The men get this, too, but being a culture dominated by men, sowing wild oats is seen as more permissible for us.

— Carlos, Hispanic, Chicago

A Latina at age 15 will have a *Quinceanera* — a gigantic birthday party. This is for the parents to advertise her as available for marriage. Being blond, blue-eyed, bilingual and with my parents having a new Corvette sends infinite messages to a Hispanic couple with a young lady they're eager to get out from under their roof. On countless occasions, I have been approached by Latina mothers asking me if I am looking for a wife.

— Kyle M., 15, white, Texas

Marrying a young Hispanic woman is considered ideal. Hispanic men do not want a woman with a lot of history.

— George, 42, Hispanic, Colorado

Latinos are very family-oriented. Plus, Latin Americans don't necessarily have the privilege of putting off marriage, parenthood and other social customs until a later age to "find themselves."

— Deborah, 46, Hispanic, Denver

We found:

"I'm surprised they gave a late date like 30. Really, if they're not married by 25, it's like what's the deal here?" said Kim Lloyd, a Washington State University sociology professor and expert on the Hispanic family.

Early marriage and child-birth are common among Hispanic cultures. A Centers for Disease Control report found that 13 percent of U.S. Hispanic women were married by age 18, compared to 8 percent of white women and 5 percent of black women. And Hispanic girls ages 10 to 14 had birth rates of 1.4 per 1,000 — twice the rate of the overall age group.

Many surveys show that Hispanic women list being married and having a family as the most important things in their lives, Lloyd said, while white or African-American women are more likely to put personal happiness or job stability higher.

"It's a bigger focus on family and traditional views of gender roles. Men bring home the bacon, the woman has greater say in raising the children."

Catholicism, the dominant faith among many Hispanics, plays a large role, emphasizing marriage and family, she said.

One new finding by Lloyd: First-generation Hispanics are more likely to aspire to marriage than second-generation, who are assimilating to Anglo views — but the third generation is behaving more like the first, getting married earlier.

"Even in my classes, the Latinas say they get a lot of pressure from their parents like 'Why are you wasting time in college?' They fight it, but a lot of them drop out."

The low … rider … is a little higher. Right?

They asked:

Why do some Mexicans like to lower their cars?
— *Candice, 52, white, Sacramento, Calif.*

You said:

I think it's for the same reason some Americans like to raise their cars [back end] and four-wheel drive trucks: To the driver, it's cool.
— *C.M., white female, St. Paul, Minn.*

Mexicans aren't the only people who alter motor vehicles. Have you never seen hot rods? "Low-riding" requires lots of time, money, electrical and mechanical knowledge and artistic vision. Take a moment to look at the mini-murals the vehicles are embellished with: true works of art that usually are dedicated to religion or a loved one. A lot of pride is taken in the final products, hence the slow driving to better display the vehicles. And by the way, I know low-riders who are Latino, African-American, First Nation, Filipino — even Caucasian.
— *Travesa, Hispanic female, San Francisco Bay area*

I live at the border, and I've seen that this happens on the U.S. side, and with a few people inside the Mexican border. But in Mexico as a country, you'll never find cars like that.
— *Mixcoatl, male, Nuevo Laredo, Mexico*

We found:

You're young. You want a decent rep with the friends. You and your parents don't have a lot of bucks, but you can get your hands on a '65 Impala and the right hydraulic or airbag suspension kit.

You're buying it, and you're lowering it. Especially in southern California.

"It's the same reason rednecks soup up their pickup trucks," says East L.A.-bred bad-boy Carlos Mencia, HBO comic and the mind behind the raw Mind of Mencia variety show that aired on Comedy Central. "It's not gonna set you back what a house costs, it's gonna get you laid and it'll get you street cred. You want people to look at it and say holy shit."

Low-riders started in the early '70s, Mencia said. Older Latinos were fixing up Chevys from the '20s and '30s, but younger, second-generation Hispanics born in America — Chicanos — wanted to set themselves apart.

The long, thin body of the Impala, especially those from 1964-67, beckoned.

"When dropped, it looked really sleek. It was unique in its time."

A few other tidbits we gathered about low-riders:

- Some trace the low-rider to the Mexican-American zoot-suiters (*pachucos*) of the '30s, and the culture's "low and slow cruising" to the traditional Mexican *paseo*, where young singles walked the town plaza in a courtship custom.
- Low-riding also is about attracting the opposite sex. As Mexican-American artist Mark Machado, known as "Mr. Cartoon," told lowriding researcher Denise Sandoval in an interview: "Why does a guy build a low rider in the first place, but for the women basically. Otherwise he would drive a little bucket."
- Lowriders have air suspension or hydraulic lift kits that can pop a car up and down — sometimes six feet or more off the ground. L.A. resident Ron Aguirre's '57 Corvette was the first to use hydraulics. He didn't want his car's bottom to scrape on rough roads. Plus, he wanted to avoid getting arrested. New laws had made it illegal for any car part to be lower than the wheel rim. With the push of a button, his car, named X-Sonic, could go up or down right when needed. Like when he got pulled over. Pretty convenient.

- Expect to pay anywhere from a few hundred dollars for a low-end, do-it-yourself trabajo de mierda hydraulic pump any pendejo might do to several thousand or more for a real magnifica belleza. Even a three-pump hopping kit, no install, can set you back $2,800.
- A "bomb" is any lowrider made from a car built before 1959. "Traditionals" are made with cars built from 1959 to the mid-'70s. "Euros" use cars from Europe or Japan.

But ... why spend so much time and money on all this? Back to Mencia:

"It's taking pride in my car. We call it street cred in the hood, just as others call it getting respect in their neighborhood," he said. "It's the same thing. Credibility. It's like 'Oh, the Johnsons, did you hear about them? They got a raise! They got a promotion!' It's the same shit. It's the feathers on a peacock. We all have different ways of doing that. The rich do it with a Ferrari."

Which vehicles get altered, and how they're altered, depends on the locale, he said. A raised 4X4 truck works in a more rural area with country roads, for example, but just wouldn't look right in urban L.A.

"You take that in there and most people are going to go 'What the fuck are you doing here, are you a moron? We have roads here!' But I guess at least with a truck you can drive and pick fruit at the same time."

Is any of this really going to impress anyone?

Hell yeah, Mencia said.

"[Employers] should think, 'This guy is most likely someone who takes pride in their work [and] will take pride in whatever job he or she does.' ... Maybe his friends who are very wealthy who have these vehicles, they didn't do it themselves ... These [low-rider owners] are the guys who later come up with engineering for cars like Mercedes. They are the geeks who take pride in what they do."

Though older Impalas are still the Holy Grail of low-riders, Mencia himself went with, of all things, a lowered pickup when he was in his early 20s.

"I had all the hydraulics, and even made it a convertible. Once a guy in a Ferrari pulled up next to me and says: 'That's a great car; it's one of a kind. I'd offer you money for it but I know that'd be insulting.'"

The O.U.T.L.O.U.D.
Method to Dialogue

OPEN UP: This is mostly about opening up to yourself. Why do you want to engage someone? Is it for the right reasons? The answers might help you figure out how to approach another person. A friend once told me the real reason I started Y? wasn't for me to learn more about "Buddhists in Asia or lesbians in San Francisco," but because I wanted to learn something more about myself. He was right. Acknowledging that has helped give me perspective when considering others' answers.

USE YOUR HEAD: Plan for the right question. Not all questions need to be the "wet dogs" variety. Stereotypes and clichés don't work as well as sincere attempts to talk.

TIME IT RIGHT: Create the "O.U.T.L.O.U.D. Moment". Pick your spots for provocative dialogue. Find a genuine opening rather than create a false one. It's often during those down times between all the "vital" discourse that we can most easily find a direct path to someone's point of view. If you spend enough time sitting in the cubicle next to someone of a different culture, chances are there'll come a time — over food, perhaps, or during a power outage — when the topic you've been dying to broach will wend its way naturally into the discussion.

LOCK IN ON THE TARGET: Keeping things simple can give the best chance for getting another's trust and a meaningful reply. Some of the best questions at Y?, those that prompt the most telling answers, are also often the easiest to digest. Remember, it's not about winning your point. It's what comes from the heart that counts most — and captures people's interest. Talking from the heart also means easing into things by letting someone know *why* it would help you to learn the answer to your question before you ask it.

OWN UP TO ASSUMPTIONS: One of the most refreshing and repetitive surprises of the Y? project is the difficulty in predicting how a person will respond to a question. Blacks do not think in lockstep. Nor do whites. Nor Christians or Muslims. Nor gays or straights. Be receptive to another's ideas. Wipe the slate clean and listen to the content of the message, not the color or culture of the messenger.

UNLOAD YOUR EXPECTATIONS: Many of us are thinner-skinned than we'll admit. When we get hit with an answer or comment we hadn't anticipated, our emotions can often get caught off-balance, and our egos get bruised. The solution: Expect the unexpected. You'll never be blindsided or taken aback by information that doesn't gibe with your worldview.

DIGEST THE DIALOGUE: Learning about others doesn't stop when the talking's over. Assess what you're told and how it fits with or departs from your perspectives. Recap your discussion with a third party to distill the most relevant information into its most meaningful points.

ABOUT THE AUTHOR

Phillip J. Milano is the founder of Y? The National Forum on People's Differences, the acclaimed cross-cultural dialogue project that encourages people to ask unflinching, politically incorrect questions about our differences.

Since its creation in 1998, Phillip's web site, YForum.com, has attracted millions of visitors and thousands of questions and answers. He has been featured on CBS, CNN, BET and the BBC, and in numerous newspapers, including The Washington Post, New York Times and USA Today.

He is the author of the Perigee book "I Can't Believe You Asked That!" as well as writer of the pioneering newspaper column/blog "Dare to Ask."

Mr. Milano is a 25-year newspaper veteran. He received his Master of Business Administration from Northern Illinois University and his Bachelor of Science in Journalism from Southern Illinois University.

SPEECHES AND APPEARANCES

Mr. Milano is an in-demand speaker. For bookings, contact

Contemporary Issues Agency
809 Turnberry Drive, Waunakee, WI 53597-2256
Phone: 800-843-2179
Fax: 608-849-6311
www.CIAspeakers.com
Info@CIAspeakers.com